Farm Animals

This edition first published in 1987 by Raintree Publishers Inc.

Text copyright © 1987 by Raintree Publishers Inc.
© 1983 Hachette

Library of Congress Number: 86-33841

1 2 3 4 5 6 7 8 9   94 93 92 91 90 89 88 87

Library of Congress Cataloging in Publication Data

Finifter, Germaine.
    Ask about farm animals.

    Translation of: Les animaux de la ferme.
    Summary: Questions and answers present
information about cows, sheep, pigs, poultry,
rabbits, and other animals of farm and field.
    1. Domestic animals—Miscellanea—Juvenile
literature.   2. Animals—Miscellanea—Juvenile
literature.   [1. Domestic animals.   2. Animals.
3. Questions and answers] I. Title.
SF75.5.F5613   1987   636   86-33841
ISBN 0-8172-2881-0 (lib. bdg.)
ISBN 0-8172-2893-4 (softcover)

Cover illustration: David Schweitzer

Ask About
Farm Animals

RAINTREE PUBLISHERS
Milwaukee

Contents

The barnyard

Poultry and rabbits

The field and garden

The barnyard

Why do farmers raise animals?

Farmers raise animals to provide food for people. Animals produce meat, eggs, milk, and milk products like butter, cheese, and cream. Farm animals also supply leather, wool, and other products.

What animals live on a farm?

Cows, goats, sheep, pigs, and chickens are just a few of the animals you can find on a farm. Cows and goats produce milk. Beef cattle, sheep, and pigs produce meat. Poultry (chickens, ducks, geese, and turkeys) produce meat and eggs. Some farmers may even have a horse or a donkey on the farm. There are also usually dogs and cats on a farm.

Where do farmers get their animals?

Most farmers buy their animals at cattle markets. Chicks, ducklings, and goslings can be purchased when they are just a day old. Also for sale at cattle markets are bunnies, lambs, baby pigs, calves, and foals (baby horses).

Do all baby animals drink milk from their mothers?

Baby animals can only drink milk from their mothers if they belong to a group of animals called mammals. Animals that grow big and strong breast-feeding on milk from their mothers are horses, cows, sheep, goats, pigs, cats, dogs, and rabbits. Female birds feed their young by putting food into their babies' beaks.

Do baby pigs hatch from eggs?

Pigs belong to the mammal family and mammals don't lay eggs. They give birth to living babies. Female pigs, horses, cows, sheep, goats, rabbits, cats, and dogs are mammals that give birth to living young, just as you were born from your mother's body.

How many babies can a sow have?

The very first time that a sow gives birth, she has six or seven babies. After that, she may have ten or more. Fortunately, she has twelve breasts and plenty of milk to feed them.

Does the mother pig feed her babies for a long time?

Baby pigs feed on milk from their mother for at least twenty-one days. When it is feeding time, the mother lies down on her side so that the babies can reach her breasts. The baby pigs scramble to try to get to the breasts nearest the mother's head where there is the most milk.

What do baby pigs eat when they stop drinking their mother's milk?

The farmer gives them sweetened skim milk mixed with a special cereal. Gradually, maize (or corn), barley, oats, wheat, rye, and cooked potatoes are added to the mixture. After a while, other foods are added. Pigs are big eaters. They also need to drink a lot of water.

barley wheat

oats

maize

13

Is it true that pigs roll in the mud?

Yes, but they don't do it because they enjoy getting dirty. They roll in the mud to get rid of insects on their skin. To make sure the pigs stay clean and healthy, a farmer has to wash the pigs often and change their straw bedding daily.

Do we eat pigs?

Yes, meat from pigs is called pork. Every part of the pig from head to toe is eaten. Pork can be made into bacon, sausages, ham, and other food products that can be cooked in a variety of ways.

How long do baby animals grow inside their mothers?

It varies with each type of animal. A foal (baby horse) is not born until nearly a year after the mare (female horse) has mated with the stallion (male horse). Baby pigs take three months, three weeks, and three days to grow. A human baby takes nine months to grow.

What is a sow?

A sow is a female pig. A female sheep is called a ewe. A female goat is a nanny goat. A female rabbit is a doe. A female horse is a mare.

What is the difference between a cow, a bull, and a bullock?

A heifer is a young female calf. When she has given birth, she is called a cow. A bull is a male calf. When he is older, he will mate with a heifer or a cow. A bullock is a male that has had an operation so that he cannot mate with a cow.

What are bullocks used for?

Bullocks are calmer and easier to handle than bulls. They are used for their meat. They grow more quickly and make better meat. Some of them weigh over a ton.

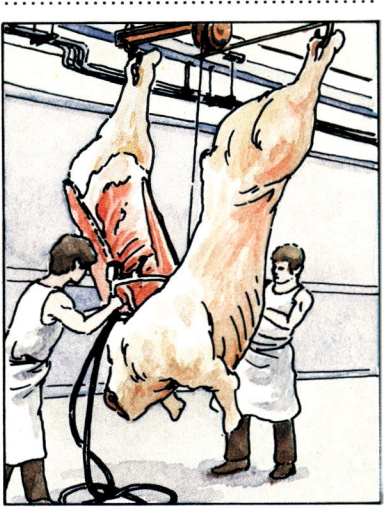

17

What does it mean when a male animal is neutered?

It means that the male animal has had an operation so that it won't mate with the female. A male lamb that is neutered becomes a sheep instead of a ram. A male pig that is neutered is called a pig instead of a boar. Cats, dogs, and other animals can be neutered also.

Where does milk come from?

The milk you pour from a carton or bottle is usually from cows. Cows eat grass in the summer, and the farmer feeds them hay, straw, beets, and corn in the winter. If they are well fed, cows produce milk from the time their first calf is born. When the calf stops drinking its mother's milk, the farmer milks the cow and sells the milk. Cows are milked either by hand or machine.

What happens if a calf loses its mother?

If a newborn calf's mother dies, the farmer has to try to find another cow that will feed the calf. Some cows, however, will not feed a calf that is not their own. If that is the case, the farmer must bottle feed the calf.

Do calves drink a lot of milk?

Calves drink approximately three gallons of milk each day so it's no wonder that they grow so rapidly. If a farmer wants to sell a cow's milk early, her calf will only be allowed to drink the mother's milk for ten days. Then the calf will be fed milk from a bucket and eat other kinds of food. If the calf is going to be sold, it will be allowed to drink its mother's milk for nine months.

Does the calf hurt its mother when it feeds?

No, because the calf grips its mother's breast between the small teeth of its lower jaw and the smooth part of its upper jaw, where there are no teeth.

Where does butter come from?

Butter is made from milk. After the farmer milks the cows, the milk is taken to a dairy. There the thick cream is collected off the top of the milk. The cream is churned in a machine until it becomes butter. Many other products such as cheese, yogurt, and cottage cheese are also made from milk.

Why do some cows wear eartags and collars?

Eartags show that the cow has been vaccinated against disease. The eartag might also carry the cow's registration number. Sometimes cows have collars so that they can be tied in a particular place.

Why don't all cows have horns?

Different breeds have different horns. Some cows don't have any horns at all because they are bred that way.

Why do some cows wear bells around their necks?

Bells serve as a warning or a signal that a cow may be wandering off.

How do animals keep warm?

Pigs have a very thick layer of fat beneath their skin that helps them keep warm in winter. Animals that live in a herd form a huddle to keep warm. In winter, cows and goats have larger and thicker coats. The wool on sheep is bushier in winter to help them keep warm.

Why do we need to shear sheep?

If sheep kept all their wool in summer, they would get overheated. So once a year at the end of spring, sheep are sheared. The wool is taken to factories where it is cleaned, dyed, woven, and knitted into clothing.

Does shearing hurt the sheep?

When you get a haircut or a man shaves, it doesn't hurt. It is the same for sheep. The sheep shearer grips the sheep firmly to keep it from moving. The sheep is sheared starting from underneath the legs and stomach. Next the neck and back are sheared.

Do all sheep have wool?

Yes, all sheep and lambs have wool. The color, thickness, and length of the wool can be different depending upon the breed. Some breeds are raised especially for their fine wool.

What do lambs eat?

When a lamb is first born, the mother licks the baby until it is completely clean. Then the lamb stands up. For the next fifteen days, it feeds on the mother's milk. Gradually, the farmer gives the lamb grass and cereals to eat. When the lamb is old enough, it begins to graze on grass. It also eats food that the farmer places in a trough in the sheep pen.

Why do lambs bleat?

Sheep live, eat, and move in flocks because they are very timid and need to feel safe. If a lamb gets separated from the flock, it will make a loud noise called a bleat. If you raise a lamb, you must be very gentle with it so that it trusts you.

Why don't people drink sheep's milk?

If you have a mother sheep (or ewe), you could drink ewes' milk. However, the ewe produces only a very small amount of milk. If any extra is available, it is usually made into cheese.

Do people drink goats' milk?

Yes, goats' milk is very good, and it is easier to digest than milk from cows. Goats' milk is often made into cheese, too. A nanny goat produces about a gallon of milk a day.

Do all goats have horns?

Most goats have horns, but Saanen goats do not. Saanen goats are beautiful white goats that have two little bumps where horns would usually be.

Why do goats butt with their horns?

Generally, goats are good natured. You can even have one pull a cart. But if a goat is annoyed, it will butt. Goats can get feisty if they aren't allowed to climb or run or if they don't get the food they want.

Why do people prefer nanny goats over billy goats?

The nanny goat (or female goat) is smaller and calmer than the billy goat (male). But the main reason people avoid billy goats is because they produce a strong, unpleasant odor.

Do people eat goats' meat?

The meat of an adult goat (usually the billy goat) is tough and has a strong flavor. People prefer to eat the meat of young goats which are called kids. Farmers usually keep nanny goats for their milk. The milk is curdled, strained, and dried into delicious cheese at a dairy.

What do horses do on a farm?

Horses are fairly rare on American farms. Years ago, horses were used to pull plows, wagons, and carts. Tractors, trucks, and vans do much of this work today.

Will horses die out like dinosaurs?

Horses are not likely to die out. Owners of big ranches still need horses. Can you imagine a cowboy without a horse? Many people ride horses for pleasure. Horses are also raised for racing, polo, and other sports.

How old does a foal have to be before it can be sold?

For five to six months, a foal (baby horse) stays with its mother and drinks her milk. Then little by little, the farmer separates the mother and baby. A foal is kept for at least a year before it is sold.

Do you need lots of room to raise a horse?

Yes, a horse needs a clean and comfortable stable with food and water troughs. A large area is needed to store the horse's food. A horse also needs a large field where it can run and eat fresh grass.

Is looking after a horse hard work?

Yes. A horse needs to be fed three times a day. It needs to be groomed every day, which is very time consuming. In the morning, you need to brush the horse with a coarse brush. Next you need to make its coat shiny with a soft body brush. Then you use a metal comb on its mane and tail. Finally, you need to clean the horse's feet. After a ride, the horse becomes sweaty, and you need to rub the horse down with clean straw so that it won't catch cold.

What does a donkey do on a farm?

Donkeys used to do a bit of everything on a farm. They carried heavy loads and helped in the fields. Donkeys are still used in the mountains or in fields that are hard to work. Donkeys are hardy, and they don't eat a lot. They are calm and gentle, too. They are often used to give children rides.

Poultry and rabbits

Why do chickens run away when you go near them?

Chickens frighten easily. They are most comfortable and calm with the people who usually bring them food. They don't like changes and become quite upset with the least disturbance. It is only their enormous appetite that makes them leave the henhouse to eat seeds, worms, and small pebbles. Pebbles help chickens digest food.

How long does it take a chick to grow?

If eggs are to be hatched, the hen sits on them for twenty-one days. When a male chick (or rooster) is four or five weeks old, the "comb" will develop. This comb does not appear on the female hen until five months after hatching. Feathers on the rooster are long and pointed. The hen has short and rounded feathers. A hen starts to lay eggs when she is five months old. When she is a year old, she can produce eggs that will hatch.

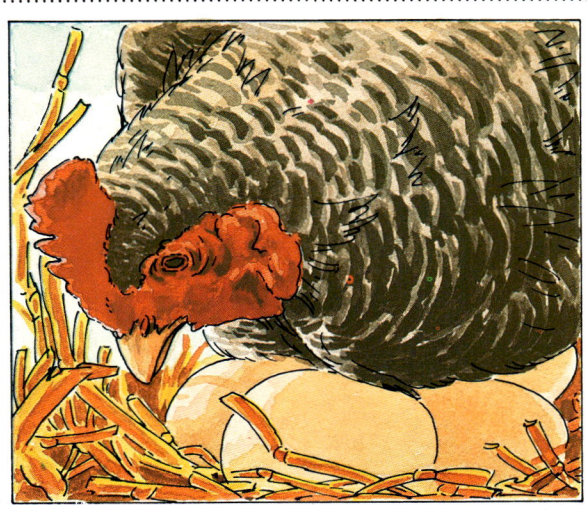

How many eggs can a hen lay?

All hens can lay eggs, but some are raised just for their meat. The best layers, however, can lay from 240-260 eggs in the first year of laying. They lay fewer the next year and fewer and fewer as time goes on. For this reason, hens are usually eaten when they are about two years old.

Do chickens wash themselves? When do they sleep?

Chickens like water for drinking, but they hate the rain. To wash themselves, they run a little water over their feathers with their beaks. Chickens wake up at dawn when the rooster crows and go to sleep as soon as it gets dark. No one needs to tell them it's time for bed. They settle on their perches or find a cozy corner of the hen-house and fall asleep.

Why do some chickens have broken beaks?

Sometimes chickens chase each other and fight. They pull out each other's feathers and can hurt each other. If this can't be stopped, the farmer sometimes trims a little off their beaks. That way they can no longer pull out each other's feathers. Other birds, like ducks, also have these bad habits.

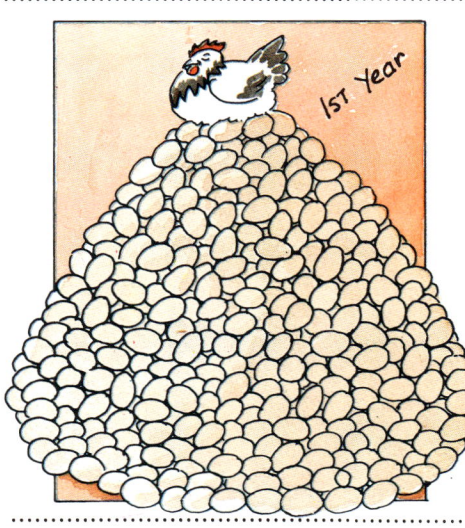

1st Year

2nd Year

Do ducks need water?

Yes, they find much of their food in ponds and other bodies of water. They dive into the water to eat tadpoles, fish, and plants. They search on land for the rest of their food. Like chickens, ducks eat pebbles. The pebbles help with digestion.

How many eggs can a duck lay?

A duck lays about twenty eggs in laying season in the spring and summer. She sits on her eggs for twenty-eight days, but not all the eggs will hatch. Ducks will sometimes refuse to sit on their eggs. Then the farmer will get a hen or a turkey to sit on the duck eggs until they hatch.

Why don't people eat ducks' eggs?

Since ducks lay only twenty eggs a year, the farmer usually keeps the eggs for hatching. Ducks are raised to be eaten. Duck feathers and down can be used to fill pillows and comforters.

Do geese bite people?

Geese can't bite because they don't have teeth. They will peck at someone who is bothering them, however. Most female geese are friendly and good-natured. The male goose (or gander) is not as friendly. He will fight with other males to keep them away from the females.

What do geese eat?

Geese feed on grass and seeds. In addition, the farmer gives them a mash of wheat, barley, and corn meal. Sometimes geese wander a long way from home to feast on nettles, but they return to the farm by sunset.

What is the biggest bird in the barnyard?

The turkey is the biggest, weighing some-times over forty pounds. Most male turkeys weigh about twenty-six pounds when they are six months old, but the female weighs quite a bit less. Turkey chicks weigh barely two ounces at birth.

How soon can a turkey chick feed itself?

Turkey chicks are rather helpless and need to be taught how to feed. The farmer dunks a chick's beak into the water, into the food, and then into the water again so that the chick will drink and eat. Bright objects are placed in the trough to draw attention to the food. Turkey chicks start eating greens and insects at six weeks. The farmer also feeds them a mash of meat, corn, bran, and oats.

What are guinea fowl?

Guinea fowl are part of the pheasant family. They originated in West Africa and were brought to other parts of the world by the Portuguese. Guinea fowl are dark gray with white spots. They are raised for their meat and eggs. Some farmers keep a few on the farm because they call out when a stranger or a fox is near.

Are there wild guinea fowl?

Guinea fowl are no longer wild, but they are independent birds who like to perch in trees sometimes far away from the farm. To keep them from flying far off, farmers may clip the guinea fowl's wings.

Are pigeons wild or tame?

Pigeons that you see in parks and in the street are wild. Tame pigeons live in pigeon coops. The female lays her eggs in the coop, and the male helps to sit on them. They take turns over the eighteen days before the babies hatch. There are many types of tame pigeons, and some are bred for racing.

What are quail?

Quail are small birds in the pheasant family. They breed quickly, and the females start to lay eggs when they are just one month old. They lay over three hundred eggs in one year. The eggs are tiny, pear-shaped, yellowish with brown speckles, and delicious.

What do rabbits eat?

Rabbits like carrots, cabbage, turnips, clover, alfalfa, dandelions, bread, and grains. The farmer feeds them in the morning and at night.

Hen's egg

quail's egg

Why shouldn't people touch baby rabbits?

Rabbits are familiar with the person who feeds them and cleans their hutch or home. They trust that person if he or she should touch their baby bunnies. If anyone else touches them, the mother rabbit becomes frightened. She may become so upset that she will refuse to feed her babies. It is best for people not to stroke the bunnies until the bunnies are big enough to leave the nest.

How does a female rabbit have babies?

The female rabbit (or doe) starts mating at seven or eight months old. It takes thirty days for the babies to be born. She usually has eight babies at a time and can have four litters of babies a year. She makes a nest for them from fur that she plucks from her stomach. The babies feed on the mother's milk until they are separated from the mother at seven weeks old.

Why are guinea pigs often kept with rabbits?

At one time, farmers thought that putting a guinea pig in a rabbit hutch would keep rats away. But the truth is that a rat will enter a hutch to eat the rabbits' food, and the guinea pig will not be able to do anything about it. Guinea pigs are placed in the hutch to keep rabbits company.

The field and garden

Will a rat try to eat a rabbit?

Rats want to eat the rabbits' food, not the rabbits. In summer, rats eat grain in the fields. But the rest of the year, they hunt for grain in barns, granaries, rabbits' hutches, and other indoor places.

Do farmers keep cats to hunt mice?

Yes, cats hunt mice, rats, and other rodents. Cats stalk their prey silently and then pounce on it. A mother cat teaches her kittens how to hunt when they are very young.

Do dogs hunt?

Dogs that live with and are fed by people do not hunt. There are some types of dogs, however, that are bred for hunting. They bring back an animal that a man has shot. Other kinds of dogs are bred to watch sheep, to serve as guard dogs, or to be Seeing Eye dogs.

Why are hens and chickens shut in the henhouse at night?

Hens and chickens sleep in a henhouse at night so that they are protected from hungry foxes. Other animals, such as weasels, also like to attack and eat hens and chickens.

Is it true that foxes attack porcupines?

When a porcupine is frightened, it puts its nose down, arches its back into a ball, and positions itself so that its tail is facing the enemy. The porcupine does not shoot its sharp, barbed quills, but its lashing tail drives the quills into any object it strikes. Animals can pounce on the porcupine only if it uncurls.

What does a hedgehog eat?

A hedgehog, which is found in Europe, Asia, and Africa, hunts for insects, earthworms, slugs, snails, and snakes in the evening. The hedgehog also enjoys birds' eggs and milk that the farmer may leave out for it. The farmer is grateful to the hedgehog for eating pests in the vegetable garden.

Is it a good idea to keep a tortoise in the garden?

No, because a tortoise will eat the plants in the garden, and it may wander off and get lost.

Do tortoises live in water?

Tortoises live on land; turtles live in water. Small, flat turtles that you see in a pond are called terrapins. Terrapins feed on small animals; tortoises eat plants. Both the tortoise and the turtle can pull their heads and feet into their shells.

Do frogs live in water?

They don't live in water all the time, but they need to be in a pond to breed. The female lays eggs in the water, and a week later the babies, called tadpoles, hatch. Over a period of nine weeks, the tadpoles develop lungs and feet and turn into frogs.

What are molehills?

The earth is pushed to the surface and forms molehills when the mole digs tunnels. Moles are not often seen because they only come above ground when it is dark. Moles feed on earthworms and insects underground.

Do moles help the farmer?

No. A farmer cannot let the mole dig up the fields because this can cause a lot of damage to crops. It is not easy for a farmer to get rid of a mole. Moles pick up scents and hear very well to warn them of danger. They have many tunnels for hiding and escaping.

Is it true that owls live in barns?

The barn owl nests in a barn or granary. In the daytime, it stays inside. It flies out in the dark of night to hunt. An owl sees better at night than during the day. From a high branch, it will see an earthworm, a bird, or a mouse and silently swoop down to seize the prey.

What birds usually nest in a barn wall?

Titmice commonly nest in barns. They build nests lined with bits of wool and fur. Titmice look for protected places to build their nests and have their babies. They may even nest in a mailbox. In America, a member of the titmouse family is the chickadee.

What do ladybugs do?

Ladybugs are very helpful to gardeners. They eat pests called aphids that can destroy flower and vegetable gardens. There are many types of ladybugs, but the most common one has seven black spots on a red shell.

What is manure?

Straw bedding that animals have soiled is piled together in the barnyard where it becomes manure. The farmer spreads the manure over the soil in the fields as fertilizer. This helps the crops that are planted grow big and healthy.

Is being a farmer hard work?

Farmers are very busy from sunrise to sunset seven days a week. They milk cows, produce crops in the fields, and raise animals. Farming is a job that never ends.

Do you learn how to be a farmer in school?

Farms can run in families from generation to generation, so that farmers are often the children of farmers. Children learn about farming from their parents. When the children are college age, they may want to study agriculture and modern farming methods at a university.

Glossary

agriculture—the science of cultivating the soil, producing crops, and raising livestock (p. 60)

ewe—a female sheep (p. 16)

foal—a baby horse (p. 10)

granary—a storehouse for grain (p. 50)

hutch—a pen that is home for an animal (p. 48)

mammals—animals that give birth to living young and nourish the young with milk from the mother (p. 10)

neutered—an animal who has had an operation so that it will not mate (p. 18)

poultry—birds on a farm (chickens, geese, ducks, etc.) raised for their eggs or meat (p. 36)

prey—an animal seized by another for food (p. 58)

sow—a female pig (p. 16)

tadpole—an immature animal that will grow into an adult frog or toad (p. 56)

terrapin—a small, flat turtle that lives in a pond (p. 54)

Index